THE WORLD OF
**VIDEO
GAMES**

VIDEO GAMES AND
CULTURE

By Carolyn Williams-Noren

ReferencePoint
Press®

San Diego, CA

© 2019 ReferencePoint Press, Inc.
Printed in the United States

For more information, contact:
ReferencePoint Press, Inc.
PO Box 27779
San Diego, CA 92198
www.ReferencePointPress.com

LIBRARY OF CONGRESS CATALOGING-IN-PUBLICATION DATA

Name: Williams-Noren, Carolyn, 1974– author.
Title: Video Games and Culture/by Carolyn Williams-Noren.
Description: San Diego, CA: ReferencePoint Press, Inc., [2019] | Series: The World of Video Games | Audience: Grade 9 to 12 | Includes bibliographical references and index.
ISBN: 978-1-68282-561-7 (hardback)
ISBN: 978-1-68282-562-4 (ebook)
The complete Library of Congress record is available at www.loc.gov.

CONTENTS

**IMPORTANT EVENTS IN THE
HISTORY OF VIDEO GAMES**   4

INTRODUCTION   6
Becoming Part of the Culture

CHAPTER 1   10
Cultural Conversations about Video Games

CHAPTER 2   26
How Does Culture Shape Video Games?

CHAPTER 3   38
How Do Video Games Shape Culture?

CHAPTER 4   58
The Future of Video Games and Culture

Source Notes   70
For Further Research   74
Index   76
Image Credits   79
About the Author   80

IMPORTANT EVENTS IN THE HISTORY OF
VIDEO GAMES

1962
MIT students develop *Spacewar!*, the first video game to be played on multiple computers.

1971
Don Rawitsch, Paul Dillenberger, and Bill Heinemann create *The Oregon Trail*, which is then distributed to schools across the United States.

2002
The US Army releases *America's Army*, a free, online multiplayer game intended to inspire players to volunteer for military service. The game is among the ten most popular video games worldwide for the next seven years.

1960	1970	1980	1990	2000

1980
Atari releases *Missile Command*, in which players fend off Soviet missiles closing in on an unnamed US city. The game becomes one of the most popular arcade games of all time.

1999
US Army Colonel Casey Wardynski comes up with the idea to use a video game as a recruiting tool.

game program™
missile command™
Use with Joystick Controllers

RI® CX2638
PROGRAM CONTENTS © 1981 ATARI, INC.

2004
With funding and guidance from the US Army, Pandemic creates *Full Spectrum Warrior*. It's played by both civilian and military training audiences.

2011
The Supreme Court strikes down a California law banning the sale of violent video games to minors. The ruling classifies video games as free speech protected under the First Amendment.

2016
Niantic releases *Pokémon Go*, which introduces augmented reality to a large portion of the gaming world.

2009
President Barack Obama says, "We need to replace that video game with a book and make sure that homework gets done."

2018
President Donald Trump holds a summ on violent video games and their effe on youth.

2005	2010	2015	2020

2014
Men involved in the movement known as Gamergate harass and threaten women in the gaming industry. This spurs a national discussion on representation issues in video games.

2007
The iPhone goes on sale for the first time.

2010
Critic Roger Ebert writes, "No video gamer now living will survive long enough to experience the medium as an art form."

2012
The Museum of Modern Art begins acquiring video games to be part of its

BECOMING PART
OF THE CULTURE

During the spring of 2018, a commentator for the *Chicago Tribune* wrote, "What we are looking at here is an epidemic, a pestilence that's sweeping across the country."[1] A *Good Morning America* anchor opened her coverage by looking right at the camera and announcing seriously, "A parenting alert. . ."[2] These people weren't worried about a disease or a wave of violent crime. They were talking about *Fortnite: Battle Royale*. The cartoonish third-person shooter video game was downloaded an estimated 100 million times on Apple iOS devices in its first 138 days, and everyone from middle schoolers to sports stars seemed to be playing it. Alarm was not the only public reaction. Data researcher Joost van Dreunen said on NPR that the game is "like a friendly game of tag."[3] A young player interviewed on *Good Morning America* said, simply, "I mean, I just love this game. It's great."[4]

Fortnite and other video games are connected to the rest of the culture. They're shaped by many forces. And they have an effect on the culture, too, far beyond fun and entertainment.

WHAT IS CULTURE?

Culture includes the customs, symbols, habits, and beliefs held by a group of people. These beliefs and practices are passed down from

Fortnite's popularity and mass appeal have made it part of culture. Many people around the world play Fortnite.

one generation to the next. Traditions and holidays are part of culture. But what about video games? Video games are connected to a web of cultural ideas and habits including how people spend time, how people connect with one another, and how people work and learn.

No culture stays the same for very long. The people who participate in a given culture invent new technologies, make decisions, travel and share ideas with members of other cultural groups, and respond to new circumstances. This has been true throughout human history. And it's certainly true today, as communication and technology expand at top speed. Anthropologists and sociologists who study culture are often interested in how these changes happen. And change is a key part of thinking about video games and culture.

Fortnite is just one of tens of thousands of video games available. According to the Entertainment Software Association (ESA), as of

2018 more than 2.6 billion people around the world play video games. Jane McGonigal, author of *Reality Is Broken*, describes the variety of games: "We have single-player, multiplayer, and massively multiplayer games. We have games you can play on your personal computer, your console, your hand-held device, and your mobile phone."[5] Each of those devices can access games for every taste, age, and mood. Video games can be silly or serious, violent or meditative, extremely challenging or reassuringly simple.

In the United States, 60 percent of the population plays video games daily. Gamers aren't limited to a certain gender or age. About 45 percent of gamers in the United States are women, and people of all ages play games. People spend a significant amount of time on video games. According to the American Time Use Survey, "The typical American now spends more time playing games than volunteering, going to social events or going to church."[6]

> **"The typical American now spends more time playing games than volunteering, going to social events or going to church."** [6]
>
> –*Washington Post, reporting on the American Time Use Survey*

A RELATIVELY NEW MEDIUM

All video games have something in common: they're relatively new compared to other pastimes, such as reading or watching movies. The first video game to be played on multiple computers, *Spacewar!*, was developed in 1962. At that time, only a small number of people had access to computers, which were extremely large and expensive.

In the late 1970s arcade games become more available. These were video games played on large, coin-operated machines in public places such as malls. In-home gaming consoles became popular in the 1980s. The introductions of widespread high-speed internet access in the early 2000s and smartphones in 2007 brought about new gameplay possibilities.

Over just a few decades, the nature of video games has changed drastically. In the 1970s, players were impressed with an early tennis-like game called *Pong*. It was available for one or two players as an arcade game or at-home on the Magnavox Odyssey. In *Pong,* each player controlled a ping pong paddle, a short, straight line that could be moved up and down. Today, the video game industry is entirely different; *Fortnite* brings together one hundred players at a time to participate in a world whose smooth, detailed, and vivid images and sounds offer a completely immersive experience.

It's no surprise, then, that the way we think about, evaluate, use, trust, and categorize video games is still under discussion. What is the place of video games in US culture? Some people consider them a harmless form of entertainment; others say they're a silly (or even dangerous) flight from reality. Still others see video games as a kind of art or a way to influence players, whether the players know it or not. Some leaders are eager to use gaming to accomplish goals: to educate students, train the military, push forward scientific research, and more. Others are hesitant to allow video games more of a place in work and school. Conversations and arguments about these questions are everywhere. And as the technology keeps changing, those discussions will continue and evolve.

CHAPTER 1

CULTURAL CONVERSATIONS
ABOUT VIDEO GAMES

When a new technology becomes popular, there's often a period when people in the culture disagree or argue about the meaning of that technology. For example, when cars became widely available in the United States, there was a lot of discussion about what these new machines would mean for people. Auto manufacturing pioneer Henry Ford said his Model T car would allow every man to "enjoy with his family the blessing of hours of pleasure."[7] But others wondered whether cars were inherently evil. The Georgia Court of Appeals, speaking of the dangers of these driving machines, wrote: "Automobiles are to be classed with ferocious animals."[8]

People knew the function of a car—to move people or things from one place to another, quickly. But the meaning and value of the car were very much under discussion. That was well over a century ago. Though some ideas about automobiles have changed since then, the question of whether cars are good or evil is no longer a question on people's minds. The car's place in the culture is no longer a subject of much argument.

Video games, on the other hand, are relatively new and changing quickly. Conversations about their place in the culture are active and

The AR technology in Pokémon Go *is a subject of much debate. Some people are worried that players will spend more time in the digital world than in the real world.*

often passionate. It's clear what video games do: they combine visuals and interactivity with a story, problem, or goal that people choose to engage with. But the question of the value and meaning of video games is open. People disagree about what video games are for, what they mean, and what their risks and benefits might be.

The details of the conversations surrounding two games, *Pokémon Go* and *Fortnite*, show how culture continues to argue about the place of video games. Though the two games have different gameplay and mechanics, the conversations about them have some important similarities. Additionally, aside from discussing specific video games, the big question of "Are video games art?" also sparks a type of argument about where video games belong in modern culture.

THE CONVERSATION ABOUT *POKÉMON GO*

When game developer Niantic released the smartphone game *Pokémon Go* in the summer of 2016, the response was intense. It was the first popular augmented reality (AR) video game. *Pokémon Go* uses smartphones' location services and cameras to display images of Pokémon in the real world around the players. Players move from place to place to find, capture, and train the adorable creatures. It quickly became the most downloaded app of 2016, achieving more than 100 million downloads within a month of the game's release.

People credited *Pokémon Go* for a wealth of positive developments in the future of video game technology. Tech journalist Sarah Jeong wrote, "[*Pokémon Go*] gave me new eyes with which to look at my city. It pushed me to enjoy the sunshine and fresh air, and to strike up conversations with strangers."[9] Health-care worker Kay Collins, interviewed by a reporter after playing the game for hours in San Francisco, California, said, "My pedometer says I've taken way, way more steps throughout the day than I used to before I started playing this game."[10] Student Brad Ensworth found

> **"[*Pokémon Go*] gave me new eyes with which to look at my city. It pushed me to enjoy the sunshine and fresh air, and to strike up conversations with strangers."** [9]
>
> *–Sarah Jeong, tech journalist*

the game had social benefits: "You'll just run into people and spark up conversations immediately."[11]

Others reacted with concern, fear, or even a sense of doom. A group of pediatricians wrote an opinion piece for the *New York Times* expressing their concerns. They said that the game "cultivates a false sense of security among children" and that the game's lure function, a way of attracting players to a location, "leaves children potentially vulnerable to abduction and violence."[12] The New York Police Department put out a statement to remind people to watch their surroundings when using electronic devices such as smartphones and tablets.

Others worried about the subtler possible effects of AR. In a *New York Times* article called "There Are Dangers to Remaking the Real as a Virtual Place," technology scholar Sherry Turkle expressed concern about people spending hours per day playing AR games. She explained, "At the end of the day, in our conversations about who we met and what we did, we may be talking about things that don't exist."[13] Movie director Oliver Stone took it a step further. Speaking at a comic book convention, he said the game was part of a trend of people giving up their privacy to corporations. He predicted, "You'll see a new form of frankly a robot society. . . . It's what they call totalitarianism."[14]

This collection of passionate responses shows how a culture figures out how to treat something new. Both sides were objectively correct about some things.

> **"You'll see a new form of frankly a robot society. . . . It's what they call totalitarianism."** [14]
>
> —*Oliver Stone, director*

Kay Collins' pedometer reading didn't lie—the game almost certainly did increase her physical activity for a time. And the concerns about the safety of distracted pedestrians (and drivers) have, unfortunately, borne out. Mara Faccio and John J. McConnell, researchers at Purdue University, studied thousands of traffic accident reports in a county in Indiana. They found that, in the months after *Pokémon Go* was released, traffic accidents in places where the game was frequently played increased by 28 percent. The researchers estimated that, just in that one county, the cost of the increased number of accidents associated with the game was $5.2 million to $25.5 million in the first 148 days of *Pokémon Go*'s release.

The New York Police Department's safety advice is sound. We should all be aware of our surroundings and be careful crossing the street. Additionally, playing a geographically based game will make a person walk more. But beyond that we can see in these responses how people are coming to understand a new technology. People interpreted facts in different ways to figure out what *Pokémon Go* meant for themselves and the people around them. Some found the game worrisome while others emphasized its benefits. People shared their interpretations with each other in the news and in private conversations and arguments everywhere. By doing this, they helped to define the game's place in the shared culture.

As of a few years after the rush of *Pokémon Go*'s wildly popular first months, the game has not yet brought about a robot society. It also hasn't caused millions of people to magically remain physically active or chatty with strangers. It's possible, however, that the game caused the culture to shift ever so slightly in one or more of these directions. The same kinds of extreme hopes and concerns continue to surface about a wide variety of other video games.

WHO DO GAMERS PLAY WITH?

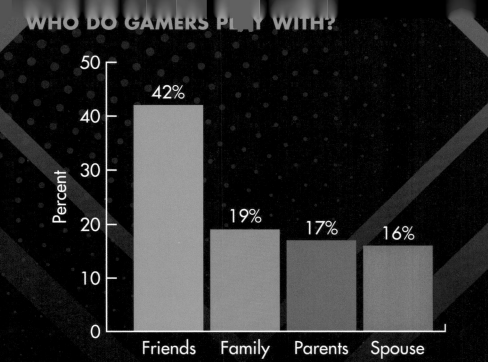

According to a survey by the Entertainment Software Association (ESA), 56 percent of people who play video games the most play multiplayer games at least once a week. This same group spends approximately seven hours playing multiplayer games online per week, and six hours playing multiplayer games with others in person per week. Video games can be a social activity. Jennifer deWinter and Lee Sheldon, in an article for *Venture Beat*, state that "the sociality of games . . . translates across countries and cultures. Players don't have to speak the same language to help each other with a quest and fight toward the same end goal."

The group of most-frequent gamers identified by the ESA play video games socially with different types of people. Some play with family members and spouses while others play with their friends. Video games help them create and maintain connections with other people in their lives.

Jennifer deWinter and Lee Sheldon, "Video Games Can Create Beneficial Social Connections and Take On Real Issues," Venture Beat, *April 5, 2018. www.venturebeat.com.*

THE CONVERSATION ABOUT *FORTNITE*

Epic Games released *Fortnite: Battle Royale* in September 2017. It was an instant hit. In the first two weeks, more than ten million people played the game. By March 2018, Epic estimated that *Fortnite* had more than forty-five million players. That May, journalist Nick Paumgarten wrote that *Fortnite* had been downloaded 60 million times and was seemingly one of the most popular video games around the world.

Free and available for a large number of platforms, including computers, game consoles, and mobile devices, *Fortnite* places players on a virtual island with ninety-nine opponents. The goal is to be the last person standing. Players must collect supplies and weapons, scavenge materials to build defensive structures, and defeat the other players. Players can team up with friends and chat using microphones or headsets while playing.

The conversations about *Fortnite* are different from those surrounding *Pokémon Go*, but they still show people looking for an understanding of where the game fits in the culture. People seem to be asking, "What is this thing?" and then trying their best to answer their own question. There isn't yet a consensus.

Paumgarten wrote, "The craze for the third-person shooter game has elements of Beatlemania, the opioid crisis, and eating Tide Pods."[15] That jam-packed sentence was presented in large print at the beginning of

> **"The craze for the third-person shooter game has elements of Beatlemania, the opioid crisis, and eating Tide Pods."** [15]
>
> —Nick Paumgarten, journalist

Paumgarten's piece on the game in the *New Yorker*, and it's a good example of the cultural desire to figure out where a video game belongs. It lines *Fortnite* up with the screaming, swooning fans of the rock band the Beatles in the 1960s. It also touches on the fear of addiction that arises so often in conversations about video games, comparing the game to the addictive class of drugs known as opioids. And the mention of Tide pods, referencing a viral phenomenon in which some people ate plastic pods of laundry detergent, shows a bit of fear that what seems appealing might turn out to contain some type of poison. These themes of fun and danger come up again and again in conversations about video games.

In spring 2018, the morning news shows *Today* and *Good Morning America* both ran worried-sounding segments about *Fortnite*. The text at the bottom of the *Good Morning America* screen read, "*Fortnite* Frenzy Sparks Parental Concerns." On these news shows and in other media, people said they were concerned about the amount of time kids and teens spend playing *Fortnite*. On *Today*, journalist Gadi Schwartz said, "This is one of those viral games that is literally sucking productivity out of schools, out of workplaces—and you can forget trying to have a conversation at home."[16] Nicholas Delean wrote in *Consumer Reports* that "Teachers across the country have complained that students are not only talking incessantly about *Fortnite* but also playing it on mobile devices in class."[17] Angelica Flores, the mother of an avid gamer, said, "It's frustrating. It's become a frustration in my home. They're so consumed in this game. They're disconnected from the real world."[18] Flores's statement that her kids are "disconnected from the real world" echoes Sherry Turkle's concern about *Pokémon Go*: that it encourages people to focus too much on video games instead of real life.

However, other people have praised *Fortnite* for being intensely social. Paumgarten called it "a kind of mass social gathering, open to a much wider array of people than the games that came before."[19] It appeals to a broader audience than have other survival games. Becca Stadner, a young *Fortnite* player, said "You don't necessarily think that females play these shooting games, but *Fortnite*'s a lot different than others."[20]

Experts have brought up several different reasons for the game's massive cultural appeal. First, for a game where the goal is to kill ninety-nine other players, *Fortnite* is relatively cartoonish and bloodless. The tone and style of the game seem welcoming and bright—not disturbing or scary. Nicole Zupich, parent of a nine-year-old boy in Ohio, has looked past the violence: "A lot of people say you shouldn't allow your children to play shooter games. But it's given us opportunities to talk about gun violence and stuff like that. It's been a good vehicle for that."[21]

Second, people like the fact that *Fortnite* is built for social play. Players can team up in pairs or groups to try to win together and, of course, use the chat feature to talk with friends while playing. The collaborative play even won over Denise DeRosa, who founded a company that helps parents keep their kids safe online. DeRosa said, "I like that players are able to talk with their friends. They have to work together in order to be one of the last ones standing, so they're helping each other."[22] However, the appealing social chat feature might contain danger, Nicholas Delean warns. He writes that "the voice chat does have the potential to expose a child to strangers."[23] In rebuttal, several others have pointed out that the feature's security settings are pretty easy to lock down.

Many games are social games. To be the last one standing, players must work together and collaborate.

The contradictory ideas about *Fortnite* stood out most at the end of the *Today* segment. Schwartz encouraged parents to set limits on their kids' gaming time. Then he pulled out his phone to demonstrate how to use the phone's battery settings to check up on kids' habits. In the process, Schwartz revealed that he himself had played *Fortnite* for 14.4 hours that week. It was in the name of research, he insisted, while his co-anchors laughed at him.

WHY THE AMBIVALENCE?

A young player interviewed on *Good Morning America* said about *Fortnite,* "I mean, I just love this game. It's great."[24] Why doesn't everyone just agree with that kid and play? Or, on the other hand, if video games are so frightening, why not get rid of them altogether? These types of questions are important parts of studying culture. Why does the culture seem to hold two opposite responses at once?

The newness of video games is one possible reason. People haven't yet seen all of the effects of hours of *Fortnite* play. Scientists are studying how video games affect kids' brains and lives. They don't have a lot of conclusive answers yet. This is a reason for uncertainty and argument.

Another possible reason to consider is that mainstream culture in the United States has a long history of ambivalence about play and games. One side argues that play and games are not only harmless, but potentially necessary. The other side says they are dangerous, wasteful, and untrustworthy. Both sides of this ambivalence can be seen in the conversations about *Pokémon Go* and *Fortnite*. Some people may be wild about a new game, while others are terrified—all at the same time.

Reactions to video games have been like this for a long time. Even back in 1983, as the first wave of home video game consoles had hit its peak, the president of the United States gave both types of response—enthusiastic and cautious—one right after the other. In a speech at Walt Disney World's EPCOT Center in Florida, President Ronald Reagan said, "Many young people have developed incredible hand, eye, and brain coordination in playing these games. The Air Force believes these kids will be outstanding pilots should they fly our jets." Moments later, he added, "I don't want the youth of this country to run home and tell their parents that the President of the United States says it's all right for them to go ahead and play video games all the time. Homework, sports, and friends still come first."[25]

A GAME THAT FEELS LIKE LIFE

Game designer Jason Rohrer thought video games were becoming too predictable. They fell into categories: shooters, driving games, fighting games, and so on. Rohrer's work changed that. His games are often ways to explore ideas and feelings. In his most famous game, *Passage*, a simple character ages as he moves through a maze. At any time, only a thin section of the maze is visible. The character can journey alone or fall in love and travel with a partner. There are treasure boxes to open in an infinite world to explore. However, time is limited. No matter what the player does, the game only lasts five minutes.

Nobody wins or loses at *Passage*. Rohrer writes, "There's no right way to play this game. Part of the goal, in fact, is to get you to reflect on the choices that you make while playing." The response to *Passage* was intense. Rohrer says, "A lot of people were, like, 'This is the first game that made me cry!'" But also, "There's also a lot of people who hated it . . . or thought it wasn't really a game."

People often use *Passage* as an example of a video game that's a work of art. Like a great novel, poem, or film, it brings players into a unique emotional experience. The curator of the Museum of Modern Art in New York City, at least, agrees. *Passage* is in the museum's permanent collection.

Jason Rohrer, "What I Was Trying to Do with Passage," Sourceforge, November 2007. www.hcsoftware.sourceforge.net.

This attitude can be seen toward all games, not just video games. In the way English speakers use the words *play* and *games* in expressions, we can see the same kind of double-sidedness. The Merriam-Webster dictionary definition of "game" is an "activity engaged in for diversion or amusement."[26] That sounds pleasant enough. But American English figures of speech use these words for less positive meanings. "Gaming the system" means working around the rules in a selfish, even sneaky way. To call someone a "player" is to say that person manipulates others. To demand, "Stop playing games with me," means, "Stop trying to trick me." To insist, "This isn't a game," means "You're not taking this seriously enough."

These figures of speech don't assume games are amusing and pleasant. They make it seem like games are something to be suspicious of. The mistrust of games that shows up in these expressions suggests a wider mistrust of games in society. Another source of suspicion about games might be the importance of work and productivity in the culture. The importance of doing something useful is definitely connected to Gadi Schwartz's statement about *Fortnite* ruining people's productivity.

THE CONVERSATION ABOUT VIDEO GAMES AS ART

Another cultural conversation about video games has to do with the question, "Are video games art?" This is another example of the culture figuring out where video games belong. And it's inspired some passionate conversation.

Famous film critic Roger Ebert kicked off the loudest, most public argument about video games and art. Ebert reviewed movies in the *Chicago Sun-Times* from 1967 until his death in 2013. In 2006, he wrote that video games couldn't be art. After that, multiple gamers, game developers, and other interested people responded, mainly disagreeing with him in online articles and many, many comments on Ebert's follow-up blog posts. The conversation went on for years. In 2010, Ebert still held the position, "No video gamer now living will survive long enough to experience the medium as an art form."[27]

Ebert supported his opinion with several different arguments. He considered it impossible for video games to be art because, in his understanding, video games are developed mainly to make money,

The graphics in video games can be beautiful. However, some people do not believe that video games count as art.

they are focused on winning and losing, and their final shape is determined by players instead of by an artist.

Kellee Santiago, founder of thatgamecompany, was one of several people who publicly disagreed with Ebert. In a 2009 speech, she said, "Video games are, in fact, art."[28] She argued that games are more than entertainment. She said games are forms of expression that engage players in meaningful ways. She gave several examples of games that are forms of artistic expression. This included her company's beautiful, non-narrative game *Flower*, where the player acts as the wind blowing petals across a landscape.

A few video game lovers ended up siding with Ebert—or at least hoping his side would win. Eric Zimmerman, an art professor and co-author of a popular video game design textbook, gave a talk

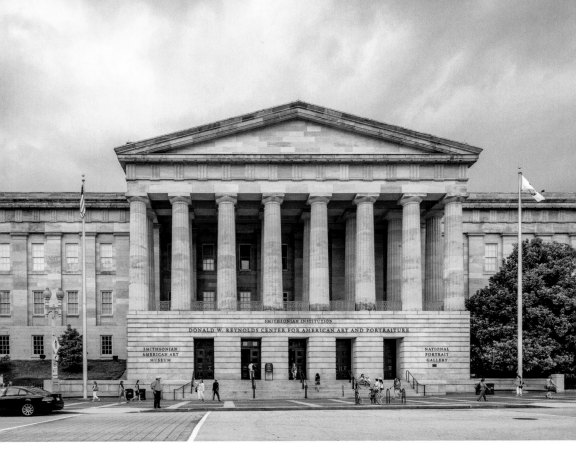

The Smithsonian American Art Museum is in Washington, D.C. The exhibit on video games included playable video games such as Pac-Man *and* Super Mario Bros.

with the title, "Games, stay away from art. Please."[29] He argued that calling video games "art" would ruin them. Placing video games in the category of "art" would make people expect something different out of games—something many game creators would not want.

Still others found the question silly or boring. Rob Pardo of Blizzard Entertainment said,

> *It really comes down to . . . how you want to define art. . . .*
> *In a lot of ways I feel it's like a silly conversation. . . . I don't*
> *consider it particularly important to me to decide one way*
> *or the other. You know, as time goes on people will define it*
> *for us.*[30]

Or, as game designer Tim Schafer put it on the website of his game development company, Double Fine, "Are games art? Zzzzzz. Oh, sorry, could you repeat the question? I fell asleep."[31]

But some people are still interested in arguing about this. It's the type of conversation that can go on and on. The definition of "art" sometimes seems hard to pin down, and video games themselves keep evolving. In the meantime, people keep making games and playing them. And some more recent facts point to a resolution. In May 2011 the National Endowment for the Arts (NEA) officially recognized video games as an artistic medium. That means the NEA is willing to give arts grants to people creating video games, just as it does for artists who create paintings, poems, music, and other works of art. In 2012, the Museum of Modern Art started acquiring video games as part of its permanent collection. That same year, the Smithsonian American Art Museum hosted *The Art of Video Games*, an exhibit exploring the history of video games as an artistic medium.

> "Are games art? Zzzzzz. Oh, sorry, could you repeat the question? I fell asleep." [31]
>
> —Tim Schafer, game designer

CHAPTER 2

HOW DOES CULTURE SHAPE VIDEO GAMES?

Video games aren't found in nature. They don't grow, as trees do, based on their own DNA. They aren't shaped, as rocks are, by the wind and waves. They're cultural objects. Video games are made by people. And people's customs, symbols, habits, and beliefs shape the objects they make. This can mean a whole range of things for video games, from the mundane to the deep.

Drexel University digital media scholar Frank J. Lee said, "Text-based games and current games are part of the larger storytelling and play that people have been doing since the beginning of time."[32] Just as hearing a story from a long-ago, far-away people would help us understand something about that people's way of life, video games today contain evidence of the larger culture.

Characters and stories from other parts of the culture make their way into video games, sometimes in obvious ways and sometimes more subtly. Video games can reflect the limitations and prejudices of the people who make them. The available technology, and who has access to it, also influences the games that get made. Additionally, in the United States, the military has shaped the world of video games in important ways.

IÑUPIAT CULTURE IN A VIDEO GAME

"We wanted to make sure the characters reflected our people. The place—the arctic. That you felt it when you were immersed in gameplay. That the colors were right in the sky. That people understood the ice and how it moves." That's what Gloria O'Neill, President of the Cook Inlet Tribal Council (CITC), says was important in making the game *Never Alone* (in Iñupiat, *Kisima Inŋitchuŋa*).

The Iñupiat, who are native to northern Alaska, tell a story called *Kunuuksaayuka* ("The Blizzard Investigator"). In the story, a child must find what's causing an endless blizzard and discover a way to restore harmony. *Never Alone* is based on that story. The player guides a girl and a white fox through a series of puzzles. The girl and the fox have to rely on each other and on spirits that appear along the way. Throughout the game, elders share stories in the Iñupiat language.

CITC created the game to engage Iñupiat young people—and others around the world—in Iñupiat culture. A group of twenty-four Iñupiat elders, storytellers, and artists was part of the game development team. Their goal was to make sure the game reflected Iñupiat ways and the values of interdependence, resiliency, accountability, and respect. *Never Alone* has been downloaded millions of times, won awards, and inspired other communities to explore similar projects. Of this success, O'Neill said, "The world was ready to use the technology of video games to share and extend culture."

Cook Inlet Tribal Council, "The Making of Never Alone," Vimeo, 2016. www.vimeo.com.

WHY ARE CERTAIN ELEMENTS IN GAMES?

The simplest way that culture shapes video games is through game content. For example, *Fortnite* was shaped in several ways by other media. Nick Paumgarten says Fortnite is "commonly described as a cross between *Minecraft* and *The Hunger Games*."[33] The similarities are clear. Like the video game *Minecraft*, *Fortnite* lets players build new structures as they play. Like *The Hunger Games*, the popular book and movie series, players are forced into a confined setting where they fight to be the last person standing.

The idea of a Battle Royale mode, involving a goal to be the last person standing, isn't new. At least one other video game, *PlayerUnknown's Battlegrounds*, used the idea first. Additionally, the term "battle royale" is taken from a Japanese movie with a similar plot. *Fortnite* draws on the medium of television, too. Every two months or so, *Fortnite* brings in new plot twists and game elements. These releases of new game material are called "seasons," just like a new set of TV episodes.

Sometimes characters and plots from other popular forms of media are turned into video games. The creators of Harry Potter, Barbie, and seemingly every book or movie make games based on the characters and plots they know will sell. From *Alice in Wonderland* to *Wings of Fire* and everything in between, stories and characters from other parts of the culture show up in video games. Disney created a version of the puzzle game *Bejeweled* with a princess theme. It's the same game as the regular version, but committed Disney princess fans are more likely to try the princess version. Countless video games draw on pop culture characters and stories in this way, and often they make a great deal of money in the process.

A pre-existing fan base played into the popularity of *Pokémon Go*. Niantic, the developers of *Pokémon Go*, had already released an AR game called *Ingress* in 2012, but *Pokémon Go* was vastly more popular. There were probably several reasons why, but one factor was certainly that so many people already knew and loved Pokémon. The Pokémon franchise started as two games for the Nintendo Game Boy, but spun off into trading cards, other video games, TV shows,

Pokémon was already a popular franchise before the release of Pokémon Go. *There are many games, movies, TV shows, and products that feature Pokémon.*

and movies. Because a familiar cultural element was part of the game, a broad audience was ready to love *Pokémon Go*.

The impulse to capitalize on already popular characters and stories is, in itself, a cultural phenomenon. The culture that makes Harry Potter video games and Disney-themed puzzle games is a culture of gamers who become attached to well-known characters. They will pay more money to spend more time with them. It's also a culture of businesses that are smart about using this impulse for their own benefit.

REFLECTING THE REST OF THE CULTURE

Video games also carry along parts of the culture they come from in less obvious ways. They reflect the values, concerns, habits, interests, and viewpoints of the people who make them. They sometimes even reflect limitations and prejudices the makers didn't know they had.

Satoshi Tajiri, the creator of Pokémon, discusses how the culture he experienced as a child influenced the games he eventually created. Growing up in rural Japan in the 1960s, Tajiri loved catching bugs in the forests and streams. He says finding insects is just one of the inspirations for Pokémon: "Everything I did as a kid is kind of rolled into one—that's what Pokémon is. Playing video games, watching TV, [cartoon character] Ultraman with his capsule monsters—they all became ingredients for the game."[34]

> "Everything I did as a kid is kind of rolled into one—that's what Pokémon is. Playing video games, watching TV, [cartoon character] Ultraman with his capsule monsters—they all became ingredients for the game." [34]
>
> —Satoshi Tajiri, creator of Pokémon

The geography of Pokémon is shaped by culture, too. Even before *Pokémon Go* turned real-world landscapes into places for gameplay, the regions in the previous Pokémon video games were based on real world locations. Up until 2011, all of the game maps were based on places in Japan. In 2011, *Pokémon Black* and *Pokémon White* were released, based on New York City. A few years later, *Pokémon X* and

Pokémon Y came along with maps based on places in France, and *Pokémon Sun* and *Pokémon Moon* had maps based on Hawaii.

PERPETUATING PROBLEMS

Those Pokémon game maps were an idealized version of the real world—peaceful and more natural, less urban. Conversely, video games can also end up duplicating the problems of the real world. For example, *Pokémon Go* players noticed that some neighborhoods seemed to have more in-game locations, called PokéStops, than others. At PokéStops players can get useful items such as eggs and Pokéballs for catching more Pokémon. It seemed like mostly-white neighborhoods had more PokéStops than mostly-black ones. Some researchers with the Urban Institute looked into this. They found the players' impressions were correct: "In neighborhoods that are majority white, there are 55 [PokéStops] on average, compared with 19 [PokéStops] in neighborhoods that are majority black."[35]

Why is this? When Niantic developed *Pokémon Go,* they based the game's map on information from their previous AR game, *Ingress. Ingress* let users suggest places to add "portals" to the map. *Ingress* players were mostly young, white, English-speaking men. Niantic added

> **"In neighborhoods that are majority white, there are 55 [PokéStops] on average, compared with 19 [PokéStops] in neighborhoods that are majority black."** [35]
>
> —*Shiva Kooragayala and Tanaya Srini, Urban Institute researchers*

more portals in business and tourist areas than in others. So most of the portals ended up in mostly-white neighborhoods, and Niantic placed PokéStops in those same locations. Most likely, the *Pokémon Go* developers at Niantic didn't mean to make the game easier for majority-white neighborhoods and players. But, because the developers were connected to a culture where bias exists, the game ended up containing that same bias.

People have noticed other ways that games can reflect the problems of the real world. Many games have shown women and people of other races in stereotyped ways or not at all. Many game developers are working to change this. But it's another example of the problems of the rest of the culture being recreated again in video games.

ACCESS TO TECHNOLOGY

Available technology, too, is an aspect of culture that influences video games. Without high-speed home internet connections, *Fortnite* would not be as popular. In a world with no smartphones, *Pokémon Go* would never have happened. Even in the earliest days of gaming— back when *Spacewar!* was the big fascination—games would not have existed without people who had access to computers.

The question of who has access to technology is also important. It influences what kinds of games are made and who can make them. For example, *Spacewar!* was built on the PDP-1, which was an early computer about the size of three refrigerators. This wasn't a machine that showed up in people's pockets and homes. Steve Russell, who created *Spacewar!*, was only able to use the PDP-1 because he was a graduate student in electrical engineering at the Massachusetts Institute of Technology (MIT). Russell and his friends were fascinated

Video games depend on people having access to technology such as high-speed internet and powerful computers. Culture is affected by which groups of people have access to this technology.

by science fiction and by the idea of space exploration and warfare. Describing the creation of *Spacewar!*, Russell said, "We said, gee, space is fun, and most people don't appreciate how to maneuver things in space. So I wrote a demo program."[36] Russell's interests influenced the game he chose to make.

What if, instead of space-loving engineering students, a completely different group of people had had access to the first computers? Gaming might have started out focused on a whole different set of interests and themes. In the decades since *Spacewar!*, access to computers has increased, and games have covered all kinds of themes. Additionally, game engines such as Unity and GameMaker provide developers with aspects of code to control the environment of the game such as gravity and motion. This makes creating video games easier, and makes it possible for many more people to make their own video games.

REAL WARS BECOME VIDEO GAME WARS

Violence in video games is a frequent topic of conversation. Many people are concerned about games causing violence in the real world. However, a culture's attitudes about war and violence may shape the games the culture produces. Of the best-selling video games sold in the United States in 2017, nearly 26 percent were shooters. Another 6 percent were fighting games, and approximately 22 percent were categorized as "action" games, many of which also include military themes.

It is fair to say that violence and war are significant to US culture. The United States spends well over $500 billion per year on its military. In 2015, the total was $596 billion—more than the next seven countries' military spending combined.

Game developers have often modeled games after real-world conflicts. For example, the game *Missile Command* was released in 1980. At the time there was a lot of political tension between the United States and the Soviet Union. This was known as the Cold War (1947–1991) because the two sides never fought each other directly. However, they often competed in technological developments such as space travel and nuclear power. People in the United States were worried that the Soviet Union would use satellites such as *Sputnik* to spy on US citizens or launch weapons targeting popular locations in the United States. In *Missile Command*, the goal was to defend the California coast from Soviet missiles. *Missile Command* became one of the most popular arcade games of all time. One reason is that it fit with people's concerns. The game's creator, Dave Theurer, said, "*Missile Command* embodied the Cold War nightmare the world lived in."[37] This same idea might help explain the popularity of later games that mirrored real-world conflicts.

> **" *Missile Command* embodied the Cold War nightmare the world lived in. "** [37]
>
> —*Dave Theurer, creator of* Missile Command

Many games portray real wars and real concerns. Some developers to go great lengths to make the details of the game world match the real world. Dave Anthony, who worked on the Call of Duty series, paid attention to the advice of many military advisers. He said,

> *My greatest honour was to consult with Lieut. Col. Oliver North on the story of* Black Ops 2. *I will never forget the stories he told me. . . . There are so many small details we could never have known about if it wasn't for his involvement.*[38]

Anthony also worked with Special Forces soldiers from the United States and Russia. He said, "Their wisdom and experience added a great deal of authenticity to the games."[39]

US MILITARY PRODUCTION OF VIDEO GAMES

There are many connections between parts of the US military and parts of the video game industry, not just the famous war-themed content of the games themselves. *Spacewar!* was built by engineering students who were funded by the US military. Additionally, as early as the 1980s, the US Defense Advanced Research Projects Agency (DARPA) approached many video game developers to make video games that could be used to train soldiers. Some game developers left the consumer game industry to work for the military. Others developed games that were sold to civilians, as well as to the military for training.

One of those games was *Full Spectrum Warrior* which was released in 2004, just after the start of the Iraq War (2003–2010). The game placed players in war in a fictional Middle Eastern country. Some of the players were soldiers in training. Others were civilians who bought the game and enjoyed it at home. *Full Spectrum Warrior* was created at a research center at the University of Southern California that is officially connected to the US Army. The army hired game company Pandemic to build the game. Pandemic worked closely with army officials to make sure the gameplay was realistic. Ed Smith wrote about the game's realism, saying, "*Full Spectrum Warrior* demanded that soldiers in-game moved, behaved, and reacted as they might in real life."[40]

A previously developed game by the US Army, which is still available to play, is *America's Army.* Launched in 2002, *America's Army* is an online multiplayer game. The game takes new players through weapons training. Then it teams them up to tackle lifelike virtual missions. The US Army developed the game because it wanted to inspire more young people to enlist in the military. Colonel Casey Wardynski, who came up with the idea for *America's Army* in 1999, said the game was targeted to boys age fourteen and older. Wardynski said, "We want kids to come into the Army and feel like they've already been there."[41]

America's Army was a hit for years. From 2002 through 2008, it was one of the ten most popular online video games worldwide. Since 2002, the US Army has released more than twenty-five updated versions of the game. Altogether, it's been downloaded more than 40 million times. In 2009, *America's Army* set five Guinness world records, including Most Downloaded War Video Game and Most Hours Spent Playing a Free Online Shooter, with more than 230.9 million hours played since 2002. Games such as *America's Army*, *Missile Command*, and even *Pokémon Go* have been created because of, and impacted by, culture in the United States and around the world. However, there are many other ways that games influence a change or shift in culture. In addition to video games based on movies, there are also movies based on video games. People may even make money and create jobs based on their ability to play popular games.

> **"We want kids to come into the Army and feel like they've already been there."** [41]
>
> —*Colonel Casey Wardynski, creator of* America's Army

HOW DO VIDEO GAMES
SHAPE CULTURE?

Culture shapes video games, but the reverse is also true. Video games affect the people who play them and shape the culture around them. Their characters, plots, and themes show up in other types of media, in people's actions, and even in the language people use every day. Video games often introduce new technology to the culture in a fun, appealing way, paving the way for new technology to enter daily life. They can change the way friendships and social lives unfold. And they've had a strong influence on education and on the military, changing the way those two important institutions—and the people in them—do business.

VIDEO GAMES IN POPULAR CULTURE

Describing *Fortnite* in the *New Yorker*, Nick Paumgarten wrote, "You may notice people around you, or professional athletes on TV, breaking into strange dances."[42] He was talking about the game's "dance emotes"—character moves that can be bought or earned within the game. During 2018, they could be seen on just about any playground in the United States as well as performed by professional athletes, stars, and *Fortnite* fans of any age. The dances in *Fortnite* all have different origins. Turk's Dance came from the TV show *Scrubs*.

Sometimes, video games such as Angry Birds *are popular enough that they influence other parts of culture.* The Angry Birds Movie *came out in 2016.*

The Fresh Dance started on the TV show *The Fresh Prince of Bel-Air*. The Floss was invented much more recently by Instagram-famous 15-year-old Russell Horning. But, no matter where they began, *Fornite* has given them an even larger audience.

Just as video games use themes and characters from other media, content from video games shows up in a variety of other places. *Fortnite*'s dance emotes are just one example. Video games have inspired many books and movies. Examples include the *World of Warcraft* book series and Faith Erin Hicks and Neil Druckmann's graphic novel *The Last of Us: American Dreams*. There are films based on games such as *Angry Birds* and *Sonic the Hedgehog*.

In each of these, a specific video game world is the subject or the starting point of a new cultural creation.

More and more, video games also show up in books and movies as what game critic Keza MacDonald calls "part of the cultural backdrop."[43] The video game isn't the subject of the movie. It's there because video games are an ordinary part of the characters' lives. For example, in *Ready Player One* (both the book by Ernest Cline and the movie directed by Steven Spielberg), characters enter a game-like virtual reality universe. And in Steve Brezenoff's YA novel, *Guy in Real Life*, the main characters meet while playing a massively multiplayer online role-playing game (MMORPG) similar to *World of Warcraft*.

INFLUENCING LANGUAGE

Beyond media, video games can also have an effect on language itself. To "level up" in a video game is to gain enough skill to unlock another level of play. But this expression has spread far from the world of video games. People talk about "leveling up" to move forward in business, politics, and many other fields.

Similarly, "game over" was first used in the days of coin-operated arcade games to let the player know it was time to put in another quarter. Some console and computer games still use it as the final screen. But people now say "game over" in a cheeky way to talk about almost any negative event, from a sports injury to a botched school assignment. This video game phrase even became part of political history in the African nation of Tunisia. In 2011, when citizens ousted President Zine al-Abidine Ben Ali, the *Guardian* published a photo of a crowd of protestors. One person in the middle held up a large, white sign proclaiming, in black and red capital letters, "Game over."

DIGITAL AND CULTURAL EXPLORATION

In July 2016, game critic Om Malik downloaded *Pokémon Go*. After playing for a few days, he happened to visit an art museum. Wandering through the museum, he wanted more details about each piece he saw. However, having spent several days immersed in *Pokémon Go*'s virtual reality interface, he no longer felt like searching the web for the answers to his questions. "I felt as if I should be able to lift my phone and get more details on the process of the creation of the art work, rather than having to type a search term into my browser."[44] Playing the game made him crave change. It made him expect technology to do more for him. And it changed the way he experienced an ordinary activity—a visit to a museum. Malik writes, "*Pokémon Go* had changed my expectations on how to access information. That shift in expectation, perhaps, is the game's true importance."[45]

> **"I felt as if I should be able to lift my phone and get more details on the process of the creation of the art work, rather than having to type a search term into my browser."**[44]
>
> —Om Malik, writer

Games often help people become more comfortable with new technology and open their minds to using it in new ways. Because game developers are always trying to make games fun, appealing, and innovative, gameplay is a common way to have a first, pleasant encounter with technology that will later become part of everyday life. Playing *Pokémon Go* was many people's first significant AR experience. In the early days of home computers, many people first interacted with a computer by playing *Flight Simulator*, *Pac-Man*, or *Missile Command*.

The writer Andrew Ervin believed that video games encouraged people to be excited about new technology that might otherwise seem scary. The very first computers were unapproachable and mysterious. People were often afraid of what these new machines would mean for their lives. Video games were a point of connection. English professor Corey Mead wrote about *Spacewar!*, "It was exciting because it introduced a whole new way of thinking about computers—namely, that they could be sources of pleasure."[46]

As Malik's experience with *Pokémon Go* shows, once people are comfortable with technology, they tend to want it to work better and improve more areas of life. Video games are one of the main reasons people want computers with more memory, faster processors, and better graphics and sound. These game-driven improvements paved the way for using computers to do everything from paying bills to video chatting with Grandma.

The game designer Merritt Kopas has written about video games' ability to introduce players to new and different ideas of all kinds. In gameplay, people become more open to seeing a new perspective. "In my experience, games have an amazing disarming quality that persuasive nonfiction and fiction writing don't always have."[47]

MEETING FRIENDS THROUGH GAMING

Riggie Medina and Christian Alaniz have lived their entire lives a few miles apart in central California. The two have a lot in common: they're

World of Warcraft is an MMORPG. Players can team up with other people to explore dungeons and fight monsters.

about the same age, and they have similar career plans, hobbies, and musical tastes. But they only met because one day they happened to be on the same team in a *Call of Duty* match. They got to know each other in the game's chat area, and soon they became friends, driving to each other's houses to game together.

Their friendship isn't uncommon. In a poll by the *Washington Post* and the University of Massachusetts Lowell, 45 percent of teen and young adult gamers said they had become friends with people they met while playing games online. A Pew Research Center study found that 57 percent of teens have made a new friend online, and many of those new friendships (36 percent) start via online video games.

There are many ways to have a social experience while playing video games. MMORPGs can include thousands or even millions of players all taking part in the same virtual world. E-Sports brings players together as competitors and as spectators. Many online games let players chat or team up with friends nearby or strangers far away. And a whole social world exists on the platform Twitch, where gamers stream videos of themselves playing video games and interact with their audiences of fans.

In some ways, this amounts to a whole new universe of ways for friendships to begin. But Rebecca Adams, a professor at the University of North Carolina at Greensboro, says, "I don't think this is such a new thing."[48] Adams has written several books on the science of friendships. She says gamer friendships follow a familiar pattern: People meet more or less by accident when they both spend time in the same place. The shared place might be school, a gym, or a coffee shop. As they discover what they have in common, they become friends in that shared space. Eventually, the friendship expands to other places. For example, friends who met in math class might decide to eat lunch together or spend time together after school. Video games are a relatively new addition to the list of shared spaces, but Adams says friendships that begin there follow the same pattern. Sometimes the friendships expand to chat spaces or other games. Sometimes they expand to physical meetups as well. In any case, friendships formed through gaming can be just as meaningful as those started offline.

GAMING AND FRIENDSHIPS

A March 2018 *Washington Post* headline reads, "The Myth of the Lonely Gamer Playing in Solitude Is Dead." A survey of the people who play video games the most often found that 55 percent say video games help connect them with their friends, and 46 percent say video games help their family spend time together.

Teenagers often build and maintain friendships through video gameplay. A 2015 Pew Research Center study looked at this trend. The study found the total number of teens who play video games is high: 84 percent of boys and 59 percent of girls. And teens don't often play alone. According to the study, "Teen gamers play games with others in person (83%) and online (75%), and they play games with friends they know in person (89%) and friends they know only online (54%)."[49]

Many people have held the stereotype of a "lonely gamer"—an individual playing alone and not interacting with others. And some past research has found evidence that video games are associated with relationship problems. For example, in 2009 researchers at Brigham Young University surveyed 813 college students around the country.

> **"Teen gamers play games with others in person (83%) and online (75%), and they play games with friends they know in person (89%) and friends they know only online (54%)."**[49]
>
> —*Pew Research Center study*

They found that, as the amount of time playing video games went up, the quality of relationships with peers and parents went down. But the researchers themselves admitted their study might not show the whole picture. One of them, Laura Walker, said, "It may be that . . . people who already struggle with relationships are trying to find other ways to spend their time."[50]

Also, social gaming technology has grown since that 2009 study. More recent research has found that, the more social interactions teens have, the less gaming is connected to loneliness and anxiety. When young people have strong friendships, even heavy gaming is not linked to problems. According to writer Christina Cooke, "for some young people, gaming is not an isolating, addictive behavior so much as a component of an active social life, like eating dinner at a friend's house."[51]

But if so much of teens' social lives happen through video games, might teens be missing out on something? One study looked at two groups of sixth graders. One group spent five days at a nature camp without any video games, texting, or other online interactions. The other group spent the five days in a more ordinary situation: going to school and using video

> **"For some young people, gaming is not an isolating, addictive behavior so much as a component of an active social life, like eating dinner at a friend's house."** [51]
>
> —*Christina Cooke, writer*

games and other technology at school and home as usual. After those five days, the nature camp group did much better on tests that asked them to read facial expressions and infer emotions. Yalda Uhls, the study's lead author, said, "If you're not practicing face-to-face communication, you could be losing important social skills."[52]

However, these researches also say that many factors other than online interactions might explain their results, so there's not a clear answer yet about how video games might help or hurt social life. One thing is certain: video games have made their way into nearly every teenager's social life, and into the social lives of many adults as well. A change to the way people reach and interact with one another is a cultural change.

VIDEO GAMES CHANGING THE MILITARY

In the modern military, video games have a part in not only recruitment but also training, development of strategy, and easing returning troops back into life at home. Even as of 2013, according to the Defense Intelligence Agency, the United States military intelligence organization, more than 300 virtual worlds were being developed for military purposes. It's not a stretch to say that video games have changed military culture.

All branches of the US military use video games and gaming technology to train troops. The military has found this economical and successful for several reasons. First, live field training is very expensive. It can use a great deal of time, space, fuel, and ammunition. In live training, people can be injured and equipment can be damaged. Game-type training avoids those costs. Second, the military has found that video games appeal to young recruits. Lieutenant Scott Barnett of the Marine Corps Modeling and Simulation

Military-themed video games often include weapons or scenarios from real battles or wars. These details help make the games feel more realistic.

Office says, "Kids who join the Marines today grew up with . . . video games and computers. So we thought . . . how can we engage them and make them want to learn?"[53] Third, military officials consider video game-style simulations a great way to teach the skills needed for battle. Scholar David Nieborg explains that, in video games, players have to keep track of many important details at once, such as "where are the opposing forces, who is talking to me, where are my teammates, where is my medic, how much time do I have left to complete the mission, how may bullets do I have left, what is the quickest way out of this hospital, what is that noise[?]"[54] Or, as Lieutenant Colonel Michael Newell puts it, "Gaming provides an ability to actually put yourself in the scenario, go through it and see it."[55]

Training isn't limited to battle. Some training games are designed to help soldiers understand the cultures where they'll be fighting. *Army 360* is set in Iraq, Afghanistan, and Somalia. Players complete military missions like in other similar games, but in *Army 360* they also have to learn about and work with local customs and habits.

Beyond training, a video game tested in 2018 adds another twist. *Operation Overmatch* has players use futuristic weapons that the US Army is building or considering building. The army plans to collect data on how tens of thousands of players, almost all of them soldiers, use the weapons in the game. The data will shape the army's decisions about which weapons to invest in and how to develop tactics for them. Feedback from gamers' actions may change the way real-life wars are fought.

Not everybody thinks using video games for military training is a great idea. People inside and outside the military have pointed out limits and problems with this practice. Ken Robinson is a Special Forces veteran and the producer of *Army 360*. He says that simulations don't prepare soldiers for the emotional reality of war. "You lose an avatar; just reboot the game," he said. "In real life, you lose your guy; you've lost your guy. And then you've got to bury him, and then you've got to call his wife."[56] Evan Wright, a reporter who spent time with US troops during the Iraq War, agrees: "When [soldiers] actually shot people, especially innocent people, and were confronted with this, I saw guys break down. The violence in games hadn't prepared them for this."[57]

TRAINING FOR CIVILIAN LIFE

The military also uses video games in another, less controversial way: to help veterans adjust to life at home after returning from deployment.

Many veterans suffer from post-traumatic stress disorder (PTSD) which is mental health condition triggered by a terrifying or life-threatening event. People with PTSD may have nightmares, flashbacks, and anxiety that keep them from being able to work or enjoy daily life. One treatment for PTSD is called exposure therapy. The idea is to gradually expose the person to the traumatic event again under safe, controlled conditions. This helps reduce the feelings of fear and trauma to a level that the patient can live with. Veterans returning from Iraq and Afghanistan can receive exposure treatment through games called *Virtual Afghanistan* and *Virtual Iraq*. These games simulate the conditions troops experience in those conflicts. Supervised by a therapist, gameplay helps them see their war memories differently, work through the traumas they experienced, and return to life at home.

As video games, *Virtual Iraq* and *Virtual Afghanistan* can reach veterans in a unique way. Many veterans feel embarrassed or ashamed to seek therapy for PTSD or other issues. When the treatment is a video game, it feels more familiar. Dr. Albert "Skip" Rizzo, a psychologist at an army-funded research center, says, "Soldiers that have gone through the treatment all say the same thing: 'I'm glad they put it in

> **"Soldiers that have gone through the treatment all say the same thing: 'I'm glad they put it in this format. It's better than having a doctor try to pull it out of you.'"** [58]
>
> —*Dr. Albert "Skip" Rizzo, psychologist*

this format. It's better than having a doctor try to pull it out of you.'"[58] In a 2008 survey of veterans who absolutely refused traditional therapy, one in five were willing to try *Virtual Iraq*.

VIDEO GAMES, THE MILITARY, AND EDUCATION

While speaking to a group of educators at a conference, Colonel Casey Wardynski was accused of using video games to teach people to kill. Wardynski responded:

> *You know, you should feel embarrassed that the military embraced this type of learning before you did. Our problem is that we end up with the seventeen-year-olds who failed in school, and if we teach them the way you do—that is, through skill-and-drill and standard methods—they're going to die. Because they don't learn that way. So we've got to teach them for real.[59]*

Wardynski happens to be a great example of the many connections between the military, video games, and education in the United States. After developing *America's Army*, Wardynski went on to serve as superintendent of schools in Huntsville, Alabama. He then became CEO of an entertainment technology company. In June 2018, the president of the United States nominated him as Army Assistant Secretary for Manpower and Reserve Affairs. This role would put him in charge of many personnel matters for the army—including training policy.

Some experts agree that video games can be an important part of learning. In a 2003 book, scholar James Paul Gee put forward the idea that gameplay is a new kind of literacy. Traditionally, *literacy* just means the ability to read and write. But Gee says we need to think of literacy in a broad way. Written language isn't the only important way of communicating. We need to be able to interpret not only written words but also complicated systems of images, symbols, sounds, and movements. Gee says that video games can be an important place for students to become literate in this new, larger way.

At Walker Mill Middle School near Washington, D.C., students in Timonious Downing's class choose to "play" the class as a certain type of character. The options are warrior, healer, or mage, which are classes that can be found in MMORPGs such as *World of Warcraft*. Each type of character has different powers and vulnerabilities. Kids earn or lose "experience points" and "health points" for their actions in class, gaining points for answering a question right or helping another student and losing points for being late or disruptive. When they earn enough points, they "level up" to receive special powers. Depending on character type, a student who's accumulated points for months might be allowed to arrive late, eat a snack in class, or hand an assignment in a day late. Downing's classroom, like classrooms in more than 20,000 US schools, uses *Classcraft*, a program that makes school feel more like a video game.

The word *gamification* was first used in 2010. It means applying game ideas and elements to the world outside of games. The characters, points, and levels in a *Classcraft* classroom are changing the way kids experience school—and they originated in video games. This is an example of video games influencing culture in a deep way. It goes beyond simply adding video games to a classroom. Instead, it uses some of the ideas that make video games interesting, fun, and rewarding, and applies them to the offline world.

The extreme example of a *Classcraft* classroom isn't the only way video games are shaping life at school. More often, games are used

PLAY VIDEO GAMES, CURE DISEASES

In a game called *Foldit*, gamers are solving one of biology's most difficult problems. They're helping scientists figure out how protein molecules work. By doing so, they may be contributing to cures for diseases such as cancer, HIV, and Alzheimer's.

Proteins are responsible for hundreds of processes in the body. Each protein has a unique, complicated, folded shape. And many diseases are related to proteins. By understanding protein folding, scientists can get closer to understanding those diseases and, one day, curing them.

Computers can be programmed to figure out protein structures. But for a visual task such as protein folding, human brains often work better than computers. *Foldit* brings the puzzle of protein folding to anyone with a computer. The free game teaches players the basics and then sets them loose with a real-life protein puzzle. Players' solutions receive scores, and players can check their success against other gamers on a leaderboard. When computers and game players competed to solve ten different protein-folding puzzles, the humans' solutions were just as good as the computer's in three cases. In the other seven puzzles, they were better than the computer's. Researchers all over the United States have called on *Foldit* players to move their research forward.

more like textbooks or notebooks; they're just another tool for learning. The game that first put educational gaming on the map, *The Oregon Trail*, was first released in 1971. *The Oregon Trail* taught geography and history by having students guide a virtual pioneer family westward in a simulation of the 1800s United States. Ever since then, from Reader Rabbit and JumpStart to *Starfall* and *DreamBox,* video games have been used in classrooms all over the country.

As the culture warms to video games, the options for video games in the classroom increase. The makers of *Minecraft* and *Civilization* have released classroom versions of their very popular games, *MinecraftEdu* and *CivilizationEDU*. Teachers are using these games and others as part of lessons on math, physics, social studies, and more. For example, Laura Israelsen, a teacher at an elementary school near Denver, Colorado, used *Minecraft* to teach a three-week unit on preserving historic buildings. Israelsen's students researched historic buildings in their state, used *Minecraft* to build reproductions of the buildings, and wrote arguments about why the buildings should continue to be preserved. Student Connor Smith did deep research into his chosen building and learned a lot. He also came away from the unit with a new view of the video game. He said, "*Minecraft* is a way to express how you think."[60]

Educational video games have received support from the highest office in the land. President Barack Obama made it a priority to encourage the making of good educational video games. He said this was one of the "grand challenges for American innovation."[61] In 2014, the first ever White House Education Game Jam brought together one hundred game developers and thirty-five teachers, learning researchers, and students to develop new educational games.

WHY USE VIDEO GAMES IN A CLASSROOM?

There are many reasons educators, parents, and kids see video games as a useful part of education. For one thing, video games are engaging and fun. Students tend to enjoy them, and that's important for learning. Gee's ideas about video games and literacy are important, too. Kids need to know not only how to read and write, but also how to understand symbols, movements, problems, and fast-changing environments. Video games, Gee and others argue, have what it takes to develop the new, broader kind of literacy.

For lower-income students who may have less access to computers at home, it seems even more important to offer this opportunity in school.

Teacher Eric Nelson reports another positive aspect of video games in the classroom. Kids love video games "because they can just hit the reset button." He continues, "That's how a lot of life should work—you make new mistakes instead of repeating the same ones over and over again."[62] According to Nelson, video games are not only interesting and engaging to students; they also create an environment that's good for learning.

> **"That's how a lot of life should work—you make new mistakes instead of repeating the same ones over and over again."** [62]
>
> *—Eric Nelson, teacher*

Additionally, research has shown that video games, even if they're not specifically "educational" games, build some important skills such as spatial awareness and coordination. They can also improve students' ability to strategize and solve problems and their ability to take in and use several kinds of information at once.

The most frequent criticism of video games in the classroom is a statement about their limits: video games aren't a magical cure. Bill MacKenty, an educator in New York City, said, "If you stick a kid in front of the computer and expect something magical to happen, you're going to be disappointed."[63] MacKenty argues that video games aren't a substitute for skilled, well-planned teaching.

The financial cost of video games is also a concern. The games themselves need to be purchased, but the larger cost is the

Students who have access to video game technology at home may have an easier time using this technology in school. They may also be able to practice using the technology in their free time.

equipment such as computers or tablets to run the games on. This also includes the time and skill needed to maintain that equipment. Not all schools can afford this extra cost. Video games in the classroom also bring up concerns about equity. Some students have access to computers and game consoles at home. Others don't. If a classroom relies a lot on video games, students who can explore and work more at home may do better in school. They are more familiar with how video games work. This could mean a bigger gap between higher- and lower-income students' learning.

WHO MAKES THE RULES OF VIDEO GAMES?

Another, more complicated concern applies to video games used in education, in the military, and in other parts of culture. This concern has to do with the nature of games. The world of a video game can look and feel like a real world. That's part of what makes video games good training tools. Players become emotionally involved with the game. They learn to think the way the game needs them to think. But no game is neutral. Games are made by people who have biases, assumptions, and beliefs. The biases, assumptions, and beliefs may become part of the game. As the player moves through the game he or she might feel in control. However, by playing the game, the player has agreed to a certain set of rules. As tech columnist J.C. Herz writes, it's important to ask, "Who has created this environment, and what do they want you to believe?" Herz also puts it another way: "If you're going to . . . fight a computer-mediated war—if you're going to play these games—it's a good idea to know who's making up the rules."[64] Who is the enemy in the game, and why are they being portrayed as the enemy?

> **"Who has created this environment, and what do they want you to believe?"**[64]
>
> *–J.C. Herz, tech columnist*

What biases might the game makers have about the world in the game? If video gameplay is a type of literacy, then video games need critical readers as much as books do.

CHAPTER 4

THE FUTURE OF VIDEO
GAMES AND CULTURE

Bernard Suits, a twentieth-century American philosopher, wrote, "It is games that give us something to do when there is nothing to do. . . . But they are much more important than that. They are clues to the future."[65] Considering all of the ways video games are shaped by culture, shape the culture, and are part of conversations and arguments within the culture, it seems possible to glimpse quite a few clues to the future in video games.

The dynamic future of video games and culture isn't easy to predict. However, certain trends and conversations point to the kinds of changes that might be coming up. The increasing diversity of gamers and game developers will drive changes in the gaming world in the coming years. Political leadership, especially related to gaming, violence, and education, will be important. New ways to create, find, and access games may change the landscape considerably. The culture will keep making choices about where and how to categorize certain types of games—and even whether the giant range of "video games" even belong together in the same category.

Many people like to cosplay, or dress up, as their favorite video game characters. Cosplayers, pictured above dressed as characters from Overwatch, *attend video game conventions around the world.*

MORE GAMERS

For a long time, the "gamer" most people imagined was a teenaged boy. Companies have long created and marketed video games mainly to and for boys. Game critic Brendan Keogh writes that women have always been part of making and playing video games, but when it comes to imagining the average gamer, "the cultural impression is one of young, nerdy men hunched over computers."[66]

Until recently, most of the protagonists in video games were white. People of color (POC) rarely appeared as main characters. When they did, they were often shown in stereotyped or unflattering ways such as Nightwolf, a bad Native American stereotype, in the

Mortal Kombat series of games. Even in 2005, a research team headed by Karen E. Dill found that "68% of main characters and 72% of the secondary characters were white."[67]

However, cultural ideas about who games are for are changing. The world of video games and gamers is becoming more diverse and more accessible. Partly, this is happening because of changes in the culture outside the gaming world. In many areas such as politics, education, entertainment, and business, women and POC are pushing for and getting fairer treatment and more recognition and representation than they've had in the past. The video game community is shaped by those same forces.

Additionally, video games are easier to access now than ever before. Years ago, almost all gaming required a special console or an expensive computer, and most games had a steep learning curve. But no more. Keogh writes, "Almost every adult now has a device in their pocket capable of playing millions of video games, many of which have easy and intuitive controls."[68] There is a growing sense that video games are for everyone.

Change like this isn't always easy. In 2014, the movement known as Gamergate erupted in the gaming world. This was a complicated set of arguments about what counts as a game

> **"Almost every adult now has a device in their pocket capable of playing millions of video games, many of which have easy and intuitive controls."**[68]
>
> —*Brendan Keogh, game critic*

and who counts as a gamer. Some Gamergaters physically threatened female game developers and writers. Helen Lewis writes:

> Gamergaters seemed angry about many things: the increasing number of women playing and featuring in video games; the sometimes overly cosy friendships between games developers and the journalists who covered their work; and the meaninglessness of 'gamer' as an identity in an age where your grandma can play a £2.99 puzzler on her iPhone.[69]

As the turmoil of Gamergate wound down, Andreas Zecher of the game studio Spaces of Play wrote an open letter to the gaming community. It read in part, "We believe that everyone, no matter what gender, sexual orientation, ethnicity, religion or disability has the right to play games, criticize games and make games without getting harassed or threatened. . . . It is the diversity of our community that allows games to flourish."[70] Thousands of gaming professionals signed on. Video games continue to reflect more diversity and reach wider audiences. Technology journalist Keith Stuart writes, "The industry has been improving its depiction of non-white, non-male characters for several years. . . . There has been a real

> **"We believe that everyone, no matter what gender, sexual orientation, ethnicity, religion or disability has the right to play games, criticize games and make games without getting harassed or threatened. . . . It is the diversity of our community that allows games to flourish." [70]**
>
> —Andreas Zecher, Spaces of Play game studio

sense of momentum."[71] *Fortnite*'s very diverse set of characters is an example of this momentum. So is the fact that the game appeals to such a large, broad audience.

Another example of the momentum toward including everyone is an announcement made by Microsoft in 2017. The company added a feature called "co-pilot" to its Xbox console. This lets two separate people control the game at once. This makes access easier for players who are new to gaming or have disabilities—they can get an assist from a friend without having to hand over the controls. The company has also created many more options for customizing player avatars. The new system includes not only a range of skin color, hair type, clothing, and gender options, but also wheelchairs and prosthetic limbs. Microsoft Senior Program Manager Katie Stone Perez said, "We're bringing that 'it looks like me' moment to more people."[72] Keith Stuart believes this momentum is likely to continue. He says it's deeply important to many players, writing, "Being represented in the media makes you feel noticed, it gives you agency, it means there is a dialogue going on between you and creators."[73]

NEW WAYS TO FIND NEW GAMES

At the end of 2017, a large group of game developers was asked to predict the future of gaming in the next five years and beyond. Every single game developer independently named "discoverability" as the "the biggest problem the industry will face by 2022."[74] Among the large number of new games each year, how will players find and play the best ones? Game development is becoming easier and easier. Free or low-cost tools mean almost anybody can make a game. This means there's an explosion of new games made by all kinds of people. Game developers predict that will only increase. According to

Some games such as Fortnite *allow players to customize characters with different clothing and items. Other games allow players to customize the skin tone, hair color, and other physical features of their characters.*

developer Sean Vanaman of Campo Santo, many great games might not get the attention they'd receive in a smaller field. Games that are highly visible and widely shared are "a fraction of a fraction of a percent" of the games being made, according to Vanaman.[75]

The developers say gaming companies will need to find a way to solve this problem. Kellee Santiago suggests that subscription services, similar to Netflix, might be a solution. No matter what the solution is, the way people find and access video games is in need of some changes. And changes to who finds which games could change the relationship between gaming and the larger culture.

President Trump held a summit in 2018 to discuss violence in video games. Video game organizations such as the ESA were invited to participate.

LEADERSHIP AND LEGISLATION

President Obama actively supported educational video games. But as of 2018, President Donald Trump has mainly talked about video games as a cause of violence. After the February 2018 school shooting in Parkland, Florida, Trump said he was "hearing more and more people say the level of violence on [sic] video games is really shaping young people's thoughts."[76] Days after the shooting, he called a White House meeting with gaming industry representatives and legislators to discuss concerns about video game violence. Years of research have failed to prove that video games cause real-life violence. Some studies have even shown that violent video games lessen real-life violence. But people across all political parties have continued to blame games for violent incidents.

News analysts and game industry leaders agree it's unlikely that the US government will be able to do much to restrict violent games. In 2011, the US Supreme Court ruled in *Brown v. Entertainment Merchants Association* that video games are protected as free speech under the First Amendment to the US Constitution. The court struck down a California law that made it illegal for youth to buy certain games. If other states or the US Congress try to make laws restricting video games, the Supreme Court will probably not let those laws stand.

Even though Obama ended up supporting educational video games, he didn't always talk highly of video games. In speeches early in his presidency, he said things such as "We need to replace that video game with a book and make sure that homework gets done" and "Put down the video games and do something with your life."[77] Gamers and the video game industry found this insulting. The Entertainment Consumers Association launched a letter-writing campaign in 2009, asking people to tell the president about the games that had educated or inspired them. Obama's biggest moves in support of gaming, such as the 2014 White House Education Game Jam, came after that letter-writing campaign. It's possible that later administrations could change their tone in a similar way.

Another legal area that may get more attention in the coming years is the question of E-Sports gambling. In May 2018, states gained the power to officially allow betting on sports of all types. Right away, many states drew up laws about what types of gambling they would allow on which sports. New Jersey was one of the first states to pass such legislation in June 2018. The state passed a law

> **"People are still a bit afraid of E-Sports."** [78]
>
> —Dustin Gouker,
> sports journalist

to legalize most sports gambling, but not gambling on E-Sports or competitive video gaming. Sports journalist Dustin Gouker wrote about that decision, "People are still a bit afraid of E-Sports."[78] This is another example of a culture arguing about where video games belong. Several other states have sports gambling laws in the works. Will they include E-Sports in their gambling laws, or will they decide E-Sports don't belong in the same category as other sports? Their decisions will reveal where E-Sports sits in the culture.

THE FUTURE OF VIDEO GAMES IN THE MILITARY

Dave Anthony worked for years on the video game series Call of Duty. After he left that job, he got a call from Washington, D.C. Call of Duty was so imaginative and realistic that defense experts at the Atlantic Council wanted his input. The Atlantic Council advises the US government about "the future of unknown warfare" and other topics.[79] They wanted Anthony to be part of imagining unknown threats to the United States—and thinking of ways to defend against them.

One of Anthony's suggestions shows a possible future use of video games. In talking about the threat of school shootings, he brought up the idea of armed marshals, or, as he put it, "US soldiers who are in plainclothes, whose job is to protect schools."[80] On its own, this isn't a new plan; many people have suggested armed guards in schools. And many people have rejected the idea, saying that adding

TRACKING IDA

Tracy Fullerton is an award-winning video game designer. Her games have expanded the idea of what video games can be. Her most famous games, *Walden* and *The Night Journey*, are meditative and spiritual. Fullerton was asked what she predicts in the future of gaming, and her answer focused on her students at the Game Innovation Lab at the University of Southern California. Many younger designers, she says, are creating a more "private" gaming experience. Their games are less connected to the internet and more likely to be played alone or shared by a small group. And they may incorporate real objects with digital ones.

One student of Fullerton's, Lishan AZ, is building *Tracking Ida*, an educational alternate reality game inspired by the work of Ida B. Wells. Wells was a journalist who investigated violence against black Americans in the 1890s. In an artist statement, AZ writes, "We aim not only to spark interest in stories of Black resistance, but to create personal connection to these stories by making history come alive."

Tracking Ida combines physical objects, such as a trunk or a phonograph, with digital puzzles. Players collaborate in a hands-on way to uncover Wells's history and to investigate current issues. With such specialized equipment, the game's audience, to start, at least, will be small: a few groups of high school students. But *Tracking Ida* in many ways represents what's newest and most forward-looking in gaming.

Lishan AZ, "Artist Statement," Tracking Ida, *n.d. www.trackingida.com*

guns to schools might endanger students. But Anthony had a unique suggestion about how to win people over: use video games to sell the idea to the public. He stated:

> When we have a new product that . . . we're not sure how
> people will respond to . . . we market it as much as we can—
> we do all the things we can to essentially brainwash people

The term video game *can refer to students playing educational games in a classroom, but it can also be used for many different things. Some people believe that different types of games may need to be called something else.*

into liking it before it actually comes out. I'd like to see the government doing this too.[81]

That conversation took place in September 2014. So far, the US government has not released a video game showing off the benefits of armed school marshals. But government-supported video games that advertise a product or service are a possibility to look out for, whether they're in support of this particular idea or others in the future.

THE MEANING OF VIDEO GAMES

One part of the future of video games is the term *video game* itself. It's easy to take words for granted. However, people used the words *video game* over and over to talk about a certain set of things. Through this process, the culture came to a shared understanding of what a video game is. *Video game* was first widely used in the mid-1970s. At that time, the category held only a few things. And those things were very similar—a handful of games that all ran on similar technology and all were played in basically the same way, for the same reasons. These early games included *Pong*, *Spacewar!*, and *Space Invaders*.

More than forty years later, people use *video game* for many more things. A grandma on an airplane playing *Bejeweled* on the seat-back screen is playing a video game. A second-grader learning to calculate area and volume in *Minecraft* on a school tablet is playing a video game. Four middle schoolers in the same round of *Fortnite* on their smartphones are playing a video game. A high-school student devoted to *America's Army* is playing a video game. A veteran trying to get free from terrible memories of war is playing a video game.

It may be that, one day, people will no longer treat all of these activities as part of the same category. Andrew Ervin, in his 2017 book about how video games have changed the world, said, "Video games, taken together, are not one thing."[82] As video games pick up even more variety and more uses, it's worth noticing which other, smaller categories the culture uses to describe them. And it's worth noticing what happens to video games—whatever that term is used to describe—and culture in the future.

> **"Video games, taken together, are not one thing."** [82]
>
> —*Andrew Ervin, author of* Bit by Bit: How Video Games Transformed Our World

SOURCE NOTES

INTRODUCTION: BECOMING PART OF THE CULTURE

1. Thomas Pace, "I Almost Lost My Sons to Fortnite," *Chicago Tribune*, April 17, 2018. www.chicagotribune.com.

2. Good Morning America, "What Parents Should Know About the Online Survival Game Fortnite," *YouTube*, March 2, 2018. www.youtube.com.

3. Quoted in Aditi Bandlamudi, "The Fortnite Craze Might Be Here to Stay," *NPR*, May 5, 2018. www.npr.org.

4. Good Morning America, "What Parents Should Know."

5. Jane McGonigal, *Reality Is Broken: Why Games Make Us Better and How They Can Change the World*. New York: Penguin, 2011, p. 20.

6. Quoted in Christopher Ingraham, "It's Not Just Young Men—Everyone's Playing a Lot More Video Games," *Washington Post*, July 11, 2017. www.washingtonpost.com.

CHAPTER 1: CULTURAL CONVERSATIONS ABOUT VIDEO GAMES

7. "Popular Henry Ford Quotations," *The Henry Ford Museum*, n.d. www.thehenryford.org.

8. Quoted in Bill Loomis, "1900–1930: The Years of Driving Dangerously," *Detroit News*. April 26, 2015. www.detroitnews.com.

9. Sarah Jeong, "Pokémon Go Connects Us to Our Cities and Neighbors," *New York Times*, July 13, 2016. www.nytimes.com.

10. Quoted in Nick Wingfield and Mike Isaac, "Pokémon Go Brings Augmented Reality to a Mass Audience," *New York Times*, July 11, 2016. www.nytimes.com.

11. Quoted in Wingfield and Isaac, "Pokémon Go Brings Augmented Reality to a Mass Audience."

12. Ruth Milanaik and Maeve Sereno, "Opinion | Risks of Pokémon Go," *New York Times*, August 2, 2016. www.nytimes.com.

13. Sherry Turkle, "There Are Dangers to Remaking the Real as a Virtual Place," *New York Times*, July 13, 2016. www.nytimes.com.

14. Quoted in Josh Rottenberg, "Oliver Stone Calls 'Pokemon Go' 'Surveillance Capitalism,'" *Los Angeles Times*, July 21, 2016. www.latimes.com.

15. Nick Paumgarten, "How Fortnite Captured Teens' Hearts and Minds," *New Yorker*, May 20, 2018. www.newyorker.com.

16. Today, "Fortnite Game Craze Is Leading to School Bans, Lost Productivity," *YouTube*, April 12, 2018. www.youtube.com.

17. Quoted in Nicholas Delean, "What Parents Need to Know About Fortnite," *Consumer Reports*, April 16, 2018. www.consumerreports.org.

18. Today, "Fortnite Game Craze."

19. Paumgarten, "How Fortnite Captured Teens' Hearts and Minds."

20. Today, "Fortnite Game Craze."

21. Quoted in Delean, "What Parents Need to Know About Fortnite."

22. Quoted in Delean, "What Parents Need to Know About Fortnite."

23. Delean, "What Parents Need to Know About Fortnite."

24. Good Morning America, "What Parents Should Know."

25. Ronald Reagan, "Remarks During a Visit to Walt Disney World's EPCOT Center Near Orlando, Florida," *American Presidency Project*, March 8, 1983. www.presidency.ucsb.edu.

26. "game," *Merriam-Webster.com*, n.d. www.merriam-webster.com.

27. Roger Ebert, "Video Games Can Never Be Art." *RogerEbert.com*, April 16, 2010. www.rogerebert.com.

28. Kellee Santiago, "Are Video Games Art?" *YouTube*, July 29, 2010. www.youtube.com.

29. Quoted in Andrew Ervin, *Bit by Bit: How Video Games Transformed Our World*. New York: Basic Books, 2017, p. 216.

30. Quoted in Ervin, *Bit by Bit*, p. 212.

31. Quoted in Ervin, *Bit by Bit*, p. 213.

CHAPTER 2: HOW DOES CULTLURE SHAPE VIDEO GAMES?

32. Quoted in Ervin, *Bit by Bit*, p. 7.

33. Paumgarten, "How Fortnite Captured Teens' Hearts and Minds."

34. Quoted in Tim Larimer, "The Ultimate Game Freak," *Time*, November 22, 1999. www.time.com.

35. Shiva Kooragayala and Tanaya Srini, "Pokemon Go Is Changing How Cities Use Public Space, but Could It Be More Inclusive?" *Urban Institute*, August 5, 2016. www.urban.org.

36. Quoted in Corey Mead, *War Play: Video Games and the Future of Armed Conflict*. New York: Houghton Mifflin Harcourt, 2013, p. 14–15.

37. Quoted in Alex Rubens, "The Creation of Missile Command and the Haunting of Its Creator, Dave Theurer," *Polygon*, August 15, 2013. www.polygon.com.

38. Quoted in Simon Parkin, "Call of Duty: Gaming's Role in the Military-Entertainment Complex," *Guardian*, October 22, 2014. www.theguardian.com.

39. Quoted in Parkin, "Call of Duty: Gaming's Role in the Military-Entertainment Complex."

40. Ed Smith, "In the Army Now: The Making of Full Spectrum Warrior," *Vice*, August 24, 2016. www.vice.com.

41. Quoted in Josh White, "It's a Video Game, and an Army Recruiter," *Washington Post*, May 27, 2005. www.washingtonpost.com.

SOURCE NOTES CONTINUED

CHAPTER 3: HOW DO VIDEO GAMES SHAPE CULTURE?

42. Paumgarten, "How Fortnite Captured Teens' Hearts and Minds."

43. Keza MacDonald, "Movie Adaptations of Video Games Are Still Mostly Terrible. Why Has No One Cracked the Code?" *Guardian*, March 29, 2018. www.theguardian.com.

44. Om Malik, "Pokémon Go Will Make You Crave Augmented Reality," *New Yorker*, June 19, 2017. www.newyorker.com.

45. Malik, "Pokémon Go Will Make You Crave Augmented Reality."

46. Mead, *War Play*, p. 17.

47. Merritt Kopas, "Ludus Interruptus: Video Games and Sexuality," *The State of Play: Creators and Critics on Video Game Culture*, Daniel Goldberg and Linus Larsson, eds. New York: Seven Stories Press, 2015, p. 213.

48. Quoted in Avi and Emily Guskin, "The Myth of the Lonely Gamer Playing in Solitude Is Dead," *Washington Post*, March 9, 2018. www.washingtonpost.com.

49. Quoted in Amanda Lenhart, "Teens, Technology, and Friendships," *Pew Research Center*, August 6, 2015. www.pewinternet.org.

50. Quoted in Brigham Young University, "Video Games Linked to Poor Relationships with Friends, Family," *ScienceDaily*, January 25, 2009. www.sciencedaily.com.

51. Christina Cooke, "Heavy Video Gaming Can Be Part of a Healthy Social Life, Research Shows," *Medical Xpress*, June 12, 2017. www.medicalxpress.com.

52. Quoted in John Grgurich, "Yes, Video Games Really Are Ruining Your Kid's Social Skills," *Fiscal Times*, September 12, 2014. www.thefiscaltimes.com.

53. Quoted in Mead, *War Play*, p. 22.

54. Quoted in Mead, *War Play*, p. 53.

55. Quoted in Mead, *War Play*, p. 68–69.

56. Quoted in Peter W. Singer, "Meet the Sims . . . and Shoot Them," *Brookings*, February 22, 2010. www.brookings.edu.

57. Quoted in Scott Nicholas Romaniuk and Tobias Burgers, "Violent Video Games to Train Soldiers: Here's How U.S. Military Does It," *Business Standard*, March 8, 2017. www.business-standard.com.

58. Quoted in Mead, *War Play*, p. 140.

59. Quoted in Mead, *War Play*, p. 70.

60. Benjamin Herold, "Minecraft Fueling Creative Ideas, Analytical Thinking in K-12 Classrooms," *Education Week*, August 18, 2015. www.edweek.org.

61. Mark Deloura, "The White House Education Game Jam," *White House Archives*, October 6, 2014. www.obamawhitehouse.archives.gov.

62. Quoted in Greg Toppo, *The Game Believes in You: How Digital Play Can Make Our Kids Smarter.* New York: Palgrave MacMillan, 2015, p. 63.

63. Quoted in Cindy Long, "Educators Got Game," *NEA Today*, October 21, 2007. www.nea.org.

64. Quoted in Mead, *War Play*, p. 160–161.

CHAPTER 4: THE FUTURE OF VIDEO GAMES AND CULTURE

65. Quoted in McGonigal, *Reality Is Broken*, Epigraph.

66. Brendan Keogh, "You Can't Ignore the Cultural Power of Video Games Any Longer," *ABC News*, April 5, 2016. www.abc.net.au.

67. Sarah Elliman, "Why Representation Is Important in Video Games," *Gameskinny*, November 10, 2017. www.gameskinny.com.

68. Keogh, "You Can't Ignore the Cultural Power of Video Games Any Longer."

69. Helen Lewis, "Gamergate: A Brief History of a Computer-Age War," *Guardian*, January 11, 2015. www.theguardian.com.

70. Quoted in Caitlin Dewey, "The Only Guide to Gamergate You Will Ever Need to Read," *Washington Post*, October 14, 2014. www.washingtonpost.com.

71. Keith Stuart, "Why Diversity Matters in the Modern Video Games Industry," *Guardian*, July 18, 2017. www.theguardian.com.

72. Quoted in Stuart, "Why Diversity Matters in the Modern Video Games Industry."

73. Stuart, "Why Diversity Matters in the Modern Video Games Industry."

74. Patrick Stafford, "What Will the Game Industry Look Like in Five Years," *Polygon*, November 14, 2017. www.polygon.com.

75. Stafford, "What Will the Game Industry Look Like in Five Years."

76. Quoted in Kevin Breuninger, "Trump Linked Video Games and Violence—But Don't Expect Him or Congress to Do Anything About It," *CNBC*, March 9, 2018. www.cnbc.com.

77. Quoted in Brian Crescente, "Video Games Owe a Lot to President Obama's Administration," *Polygon*, January 20, 2017. www.polygon.com.

78. Dustin Gouker, "Will Other States Follow New Jersey's Lead on These Three Parts of Its Sports Betting Law?" *Legal Sports Report*, June 11, 2018. www.legalsportsreport.com.

79. Quoted in Simon Parkin, "Call of Duty: Gaming's Role in the Military-Entertainment Complex," *Guardian*, October 22, 2014. www.theguardian.com.

80. Quoted in Parkin, "Call of Duty: Gaming's Role in the Military-Entertainment Complex."

81. Quoted in Parkin, "Call of Duty: Gaming's Role in the Military-Entertainment Complex."

82. Ervin, *Bit by Bit*, p. 220.

FOR FURTHER RESEARCH

BOOKS

Andrew Ervin, *Bit by Bit: How Video Games Transformed Our World.*
New York: Basic Books, 2017.

Daniel Goldberg and Linus Larsson, eds., *The State of Play: Creators and Critics on Video Game Culture.* New York: Seven Stories Press, 2015.

Kathryn Hulick, *Cyber Nation: How the Digital Revolution is Changing Society.* San Diego, CA: ReferencePoint Press, 2018.

Jane McGonigal, *Reality Is Broken: Why Games Make Us Better and How They Can Change the World.* New York: Penguin, 2011.

Ashley Strehle Hartman, *Youth and Video Games.* San Diego, CA: ReferencePoint Press, 2019.

INTERNET SOURCES

Shiva Kooragayala and Tanaya Srini, "Pokémon Go Is Changing How Cities Use Public Space, But Could It Be More Inclusive?" *Urban Institute*, August 5, 2016. www.urban.org.

Helen Lewis, "Gamergate: A Brief History of a Computer-Age War," *Guardian,* January 11, 2015. www.theguardian.com.

Avi Selk and Emily Guskin, "The Myth of the Lonely Gamer Playing in Solitude Is Dead," *Washington Post*, March 9, 2018. www.washingtonpost.com.

Patrick Stafford, "What Will the Game Industry Look Like in Five Years," *Polygon*, November 14, 2017. www.polygon.com.

Keith Stuart, "Why Diversity Matters in the Modern Video Games Industry," *Guardian*, July 18, 2017. www.theguardian.com

RELATED ORGANIZATIONS AND WEBSITES

Classcraft

www.classcraft.com

Classcraft is a system that applies game principles to the classroom either for free or on a paid plan. This system helps teachers gamify their lesson plans.

Entertainment Software Association

601 Massachusetts Ave. NW, Suite 300
Washington, D.C. 20001
www.theesa.com

The Entertainment Software Organization (ESA) is an organization that represents the US video game industry.

Games for Change

www.gamesforchange.org

Games for Change connects people who make games that "help people learn, improve their communities, and contribute to make the world a better place."

International Society for Technology in Education

www.iste.org

The International Society for Technology in Education (ISTE) is a global organization that connects educators who are passionate about technology in education. The organization helps people with evidence-based learning strategies and creates a community of like-minded educators to gather resources and share ideas.

INDEX

Adams, Rebecca, 44

Air Force, US, 20

America's Army, 36–37, 51, 69

American Time Use Survey, 8

Angry Birds, 39

Anthony, Dave, 35, 66–68

Army, US, 36–37, 49, 50–51

art, 9, 11, 21, 22–25, 41, 67

augmented reality (AR), 12, 28, 31, 42

AZ, Lishan, 67

Barnett, Lieutenant Scott, 47–48

Beatles, 16–17

Bejeweled, 28, 69

Blizzard Entertainment, 24

Brezenoff, Steve, 40

Brigham Young University, 45–46

Brown v. Entertainment Merchants Association, 65

Call of Duty, 35, 43, 66

Chicago Sun-Times, 22

Chicago Tribune, 6

Cline, Ernest, 40

Cold War, 34–35

Collins, Kay, 12, 14

Congress, US, 65

Consumer Reports, 17

Cook Inlet Tribal Council (CITC), 27

Cooke, Christina, 46

Defense Advanced Research Projects Agency (DARPA), 36

Defense Intelligence Agency, 47

Delean, Nicholas, 17, 18

DeRosa, Denise, 18

deWinter, Jennifer, 15

Dill, Karen E., 60

Downing, Timonious, 52

Drexel University, 26

Druckmann, Neil, 39

E-Sports, 44, 65–66

Ebert, Roger, 22–23

education, 38, 51–56, 57, 58, 60

educational video games, 53–54, 55, 64–65, 67

   CivilizationEDU, 53–54

   Classcraft, 52

   DreamBox, 53

   JumpStart, 53

   MinecraftEdu, 53–54

   Oregon Trail, The, 53

   Reader Rabbit, 53

   Starfall, 53

Ensworth, Brad, 12–13

Entertainment Consumers Association, 65

Entertainment Software Association (ESA), 7–8, 15

Epic Games, 16

Ervin, Andrew, 42, 69

Faccio, Mara, 14

First Amendment, 65

Flight Simulator, 42

Flores, Angelica, 17

Flower, 23

Foldit, 53

Ford, Henry, 10

Fortnite: Battle Royale, 6, 7, 9, 11, 16–20, 22, 27–28, 32, 38–39, 62, 69

Full Spectrum Warrior, 36

Fullerton, Tracy, 67

gambling, 65–66
Game Boy, 28
game engines, 33–34
Gamergate, 60–61
Gee, James Paul, 51–52, 54
Georgia Court of Appeals, 10
Good Morning America, 6, 17, 19
Gouker, Dustin, 66
Guardian, 40
Guy in Real Life, 40

Herz, J.C., 57
Hicks, Faith Erin, 39
Horning, Russell, 39
Hunger Games, The, 27

Ingress, 28, 31–32
Iraq War, 36, 49, 50
Israelsen, Laura, 54

Jeong, Sarah, 12

Keogh, Brendan, 59, 60
Kopas, Merritt, 42

Last of Us: American Dreams, The, 39
Lee, Frank J., 26
Lewis, Helen, 61

MacDonald, Keza, 40
MacKenty, Bill, 55
Magnavox Odyssey, 9
Malik, Om, 41, 42
Massachusetts Institute of Technology (MIT), 32
massively multiplayer online role-playing game (MMORPG), 40, 44, 52
McConnell, John J., 14
McGonigal, Jane, 8

Mead, Corey, 42
Merriam-Webster, 21
military, US, 9, 26, 34–37, 38, 47–51, 57, 66
Minecraft, 27, 53, 54, 69
Missile Command, 34–35, 37, 42
Mortal Kombat, 59–60
Museum of Modern Art, 21, 25

National Endowment for the Arts (NEA), 25
Nelson, Eric, 55
Netflix, 63
Never Alone (*Kisima Innitchuna*), 27
New York Police Department, 13, 14
New York Times, 13
New Yorker, 17, 38
Newell, Lieutenant Colonel Michael, 48
Niantic, 12, 28, 31–32
Nieborg, David, 48
Nightwolf, 59
NPR, 6

Obama, Barack, 54, 64, 65
O'Neill, Gloria, 27
Operation Overmatch, 49

Pac-Man, 42
Pardo, Rob, 24
Passage, 21
Paumgarten, Nick, 16–17, 18, 27, 38
Perez, Katie Stone, 62
Pew Research Center, 44, 45
PlayerUnknown's Battlegrounds, 28
Pokémon, 28–29, 30–31
Pokémon Go, 11, 12–14, 16, 17, 20, 28–29, 30–32, 37, 41, 42
PokéStops, 31–32

INDEX CONTINUED

Pong, 9, 69

post-traumatic stress disorder (PTSD), 50–51

Purdue University, 14

Ready Player One, 40

Reagan, Ronald, 20

Rizzo, Albert "Skip," 50–51

Robinson, Ken, 49

Rohrer, Jason, 21

Russell, Steve, 32–33

Russia, 35

Santiago, Kellee, 23, 63

Schafer, Tim, 25

Schwartz, Gadi, 17, 19, 22

Sheldon, Lee, 15

Smith, Connor, 54

Smith, Ed, 36

Smithsonian American Art Museum, 25

Sonic the Hedgehog, 39

Space Invaders, 69

Spaces of Play, 61

Spacewar!, 8–9, 32–33, 35–36, 42, 69

Spielberg, Steven, 40

Sputnik, 34

Stadner, Becca, 18

Stone, Oliver, 13

Stuart, Keith, 61, 62

Suits, Bernard, 58

Supreme Court, US, 65

Tajiri, Satoshi, 30

thatgamecompany, 23

Today, 17, 19

Tracking Ida, 67

Trump, Donald, 64

Tunisia, 40

Turkle, Sherry, 13, 17

University of Massachusetts Lowell, 43–44

University of North Carolina at Greensboro, 44

University of Southern California, 36, 67

Vanaman, Sean, 63

Venture Beat, 15

Virtual Afghanistan, 50–51

Virtual Iraq, 50–51

virtual reality, 40, 41

Walker, Laura, 46

Walt Disney World, 20

Wardynski, Colonel Casey, 36, 51

Washington Post, 43–44, 45

White House Education Game Jam, 54, 65

World of Warcraft, 39, 40, 52

Wright, Evan, 49

Xbox, 62

Zecher, Andreas, 61

Zimmerman, Eric, 23–24

Zupich, Nicole, 18

ABOUT THE AUTHOR

Carolyn Williams-Noren writes poems and lyric essays in addition to nonfiction books for young people. She sunk quite a few hours into *Super Mario Bros. 2* as a teen. She lives in Minneapolis, Minnesota, with her husband (who, at one time, played a fair amount of *Quake*) and two daughters who enjoy *Minecraft* and *The Sims*. Carolyn has an MA in Anthropology from the University of Michigan.